# 2020 Hindsight

**Contra-Verse**
**Political + Satirical = Hysterical**

**45 *MORE* poems to read**
**on the toilet, or with a cup of**
**"COVFEFE"**

**By Victoria R. Crosby**

# 2020 Hindsight

Copyright © 2020 by Victoria R. Crosby

**Published by Tender Fire Books**

For information contact: TenderFireBooks@gmail.com

Quantity Sales available.
For details contact the publisher at the email address above.

Printed in the United States of America

ISBN: 978-1-7351238-1-3

Title: 2020 Hindsight

Library of Congress

Case # 1-8899354851

101 Independence Avenue
Washington, DC 20559-6000

First Edition: June, 2020

# ~ Dedication ~

As in "America Wake Up," I dedicate this book to my four
sons, three grandchildren, and all children of the world, in the
fervent hope that we leave you and your children and all future
generations, a much healthier world in which to live.

"I disapprove of what you say, but I will defend to the death your right to say it."

- Voltaire

Tender Fire Books

www.TenderFireBooks.com

# Foreword

Poetry expresses powerful emotions and ideas with an economy of words. It is arguably the mostly highly evolved form of written communication, requiring levels of talent and discipline that discourage most writers. A select few pursue the craft, hoping to create a work that will leave a mark on the reader, creating a bond between poet and reader that empowers both. The challenge is enormous, but the payoff is greater still.

I stand in awe of poets. I have written two books, one of which was a *New York Times* bestseller, and dozens of op-eds, but never a poem. The closest I have come is song lyrics, which aspire to poetry, but in my case generally fall short of the mark. But I have come to know this: no matter the form, each composition is an extension of the author. It is a child, if you will, which goes out into the world and reaches other people, including total strangers, in the hope of sharing something of value.

I know Victoria Crosby because I play in two bands with her third son, Jason. She is authentic. Larger than life. Her warmth envelops everyone she encounters. She is courageous, which is essential for every author. Once the publisher prints a book, the words cannot be changed, so you have to say what you mean and be able to live with that. Victoria Crosby has that skill.

I do not know how many poets have written about politics, but it is fertile ground for humor, which is the focus of this volume. The timing could not be better. Historians may classify 2020 with the most impactful years in American history, such as 1787, 1860, and 1933. In this chaotic time, when a pandemic, an economic contraction, and a presidential election take turns disorienting us all, the humorous poetry of Victoria Crosby provides welcome relief, a way to cope with the sometimes overwhelming events of our time. I hope you will enjoy it as much as I do.

**Roger McNamee- June 27, 2020**

# Introduction

My hope is that this book will entertain and inspire readers to be the change in the world that we need.

---

*"Trumpery," a word defined in the dictionary*

*as fraudulent and calculated to deceive.*

*Worthless, of no value, whose words you can't believe;*

*trifles, rubbish, and of no use to anyone at all,*

*nonsense, trashy, flashy and headed for a fall.*

---

# Index of Poems

# The Orange Thing

Ever since he rode that escalator
as though he were a gladiator
entering the ring,
that orange treasonous traitor
has been acting like a clown.
We are so grateful to Nancy Pelosi
for trying to bring him down.
No matter how many slick lawyers he hires,
and how many of those liars
twist the truth and claim fake news,
the legal system
to abuse.
The fact is that
we know darn well
that he and his
henchmen are as
guilty as hell.
Impeached he
will forever be,
and will go down
in history
as the worst leader
this country has
ever known,
as he tried to take
America as his own.

# Crime After Crime

#45 is a Christian, at least that is his claim,
but a book of the bible he simply cannot name.
He hardly attends church at all, this we know is true,
and if he does, which denomination does he belong to?
A great businessman he also claims to be,
yet so many of his businesses have been in bankruptcy.
Not to mention those fraudulent endeavors,
like his University and Trump Airlines,
for which he had to pay tremendous fines.
He says he is a patriot, but dodged the draft five times,
and these are just a few of his many crimes.
He says he is a billionaire, but won't release his tax returns,
and when he is forced to,
we will see that the money that he earns
is through his dirty dealings with many foreign powers,
who blackmail him with tapes of golden showers.
He says he is a stable genius,
but his grades he will not show,
he is not a great scholar, that we all know.
He doesn't read, he cannot spell,
he doesn't speak very well.
We don't need to see his grades to understand
that he's *not* the smartest in the land.

---

*"Actually, throughout my life, my two greatest assets have been mental stability and being, like, really smart."*

**- Donald Trump**

# It's Not My Fault

#45 says he takes no responsibility
for the virus that is affecting the country,
afraid that it would cost him the election
if he dealt with the problems of this infection.
But he has blood on his hands
as it sweeps through the lands.
He destroyed the department
that was designed to deal
with this pandemic, that is truly real.
Joking that it only affects states that are blue,
and suggesting the red state are immune to
this disease that has people sick and dying,
while #45 isn't even trying
to calm the nation like a true leader should.
Past presidents in times of crisis would
address the nation
to assure them of steps being taken,
so fear and panic didn't rule the day.
Yet #45 in his bumbling way
only instills greater fear and dread
that we are all going to end up dead!

*"The buck stops here."*

**- Harry Truman**

*"No, I don't take responsibility at all."*

## - Donald Trump

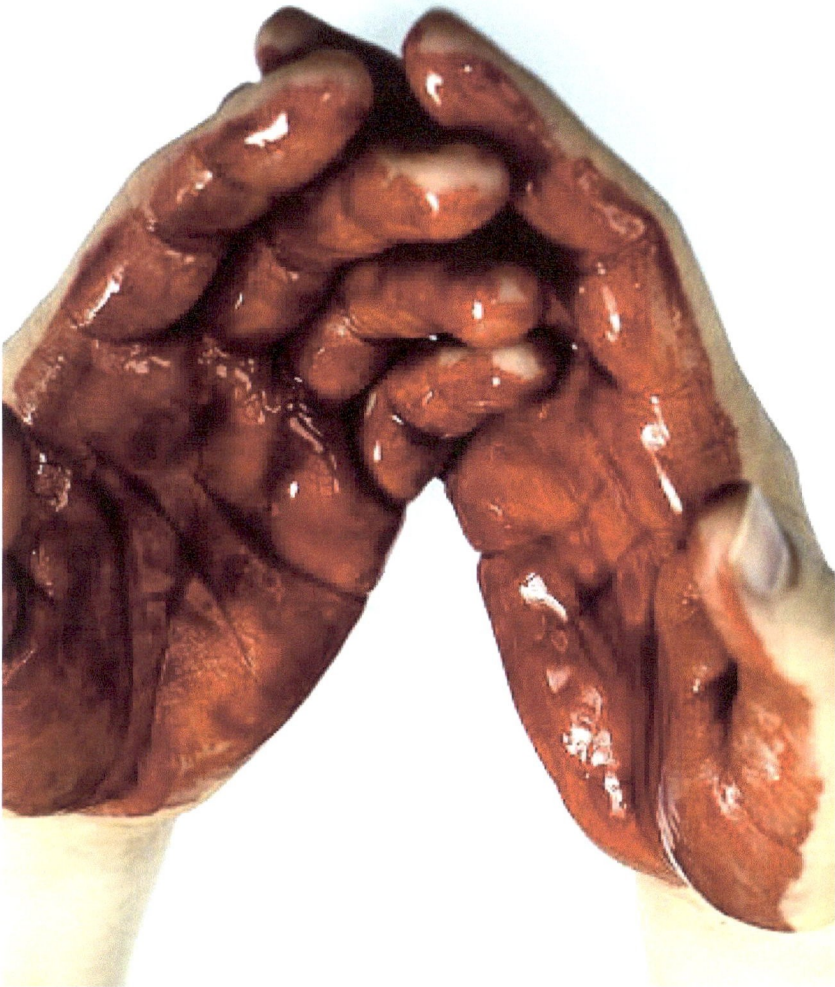

# Don The Con

#45 and his cohorts want older people to die,
as they think it will make the stock market go way up high.
Return to work, is his plea, in order to save the economy.
But he doesn't seem to realize that
as the virus spreads it doesn't care
if you're old and poor, or a young billionaire.
Your national origin and ethnicity
has no bearing on how sick you will be
once you're infected, and could then affect others,
including your parents, children, sisters and brothers,
your co-workers and everyone you come in contact with,
you could potentially give
the virus that could cause their demise.

People whose immune systems are compromised
are at the greatest risk, as everyone tries
to hoard food and supplies.
Don't buy in a panic, just take what you need,
don't let yourself be fueled by greed.
And don't listen to #45's lies,
don't put the economy before your health,
don't contribute to the greedy politicians wealth.
They will give bailouts to every big corporation
before considering the health of the people of this nation.

# He Just Doesn't Care

Not one word of sympathy has been said
by the man with the orange face and head.
Not one tear has he shed
for the many people who are now dead.
Nor for those who are sick and dying,
or for their families who are crying,
but can't hold their loved ones hand
as they cross over to the promised land,
and can't hold a funeral or service in memory
of friends, or members of their family.

We need leaders who show they truly care,
not someone who only wants to enrich himself,
and every other millionaire.
It doesn't cost anything to show sympathy,
but #45 is incapable of empathy.
He is a sociopath who has no feeling or emotion,
and his only devotion is to himself and his legacy.

---

"Sociopaths are attracted to politics because they see it as a Sphere in which you can be ruthless and step all over people. The fact that some politicians tell such awful lies is another example of sociopathy. Sociopaths lie, they see nothing wrong with it."

**- Alexander McCall Smith,**
**Professor of Medical Law**

# No Quid Pro Quo?

To the governors of each blue state
#45 said they would have to wait
for ventilators that peoples' lives would save,
although #45 would rather see them in the grave.
He said that it is a two-way street
if this virus you want to defeat.
#45 asks that each governor "treat him nice"
and is willing to sacrifice
the lives of citizens who will die
if their governors don't comply.

He wants them all down on their knees
and asking #45 with a "pretty please."
If this is not Quid Pro Quo,
what would you call it I'd like to know?
Extortion is a word that comes to mind.
And in a short time #45 will find
himself and his evil cohorts in jail,
for their greed and hubris is beyond the pale!

*"I'm not interested in power for power's sake, but I'm interested in power that is moral, that is right and that is good.*

**- Martin Luther King, Jr.**

# 2020 Heroes

The true heroes of this
world-wide crisis of health
are not the politicians, who only
seek to increase their wealth.
Not the so-called leaders,
although there are some who appear
to have qualities of leadership and seem sincere,
but the doctors, nurses and workers in health care,
the people in supermarkets and
food stores who work there.
The restaurants that prepare meals for
delivery and take-out,
let's give them all a thank you shout out.
The EMS workers, firefighters and police,
postal workers and UPS,
without all of them we'd be in a right old mess.
The workers in the field of sanitation,
all these people working with great dedication
to keep our lives as normal as can be expected,
as we try not to become infected.
The neighbors who shop for the immune compromised
and the elderly, who may not have realized
the importance of sheltering in place,
washing hands, and not touching your face.
Friends who call to check to make sure everyone is fine,
or send them an email
from time to time.
With grateful hearts we
thank you, and want
to say, you are all our
heroes, God Bless you
today, and every day.

# Empty Churches

"Go back to work by Easter" that's what #45 said
he wants to see the economy improve,
even though many may end up dead.
"Fill the churches" was his cry,
but the religious leaders know why
that is a foolish thing to say,
as this virus just won't go away
as long as people continue to congregate,
and spread the virus in every state.
Stay at home unless your work is really essential,
like those who provide services that are fundamental
to our survival; people in the medical field
who wear masks to shield them from infection,
and food providers, who also need protection.
We all need their services to survive,
they provide the necessities to keep us all alive.
If you have to go out, keep a distance of six feet
from any other people you may meet.
Wash your hands frequently and wear a mask,
don't touch your face; it's not a difficult task.
Those of you who are wiser will also use a hand sanitizer.
This virus can only be defeated once these
rules have been completed.

*"Let's lift the lockdown and pack the churches for Easter."*

**- Donald Trump**
*March 24, 2020*

# tRump *is* the Virus

#45 doesn't give a damn
that more have died of the virus than died in Viet Nam.
He is only interested in self-aggrandization
as he spreads his narcissism across the nation.
He is showing his true colors, he is just a TV entertainer.
That he has poor leadership skills is a no brainer.
He says his daily briefings of the health crisis in the USA
increase his ratings day by day.
He said his TV rating just grows and grows
and that it's as high as popular TV shows.

Governor Cuomo on the other hand
has shown qualities of leadership throughout the land,
as have some other politicians in other states,
but this kind of political management that #45 hates.
He wants to be the only one in control,
while the country sinks deeper into the hole.
He says that if we can keep the death count down
to a few hundred thou, he will have done his job very well.
Is he kidding, this orange clown?
There is a special place in hell
for his lack of compassion and caring,
with no concern about how the people are faring.

# My Corona

tRump has accused health care works of stealing
desperately needed supplies,
of course this isn't true, it's just another of his lies.
He says they are hoarding or selling at a profit
masks and ventilators and items that they need.
#45 is just projecting his own avaristic greed.
He rejected tests developed by W.H.O.
and the reason why we now know,
is because he wants his own tRump brand
that he can sell throughout the land.
He also wants his own brand of vaccine.
His money-grubbing plans are quite obscene.
His daily briefings are like an infomercial
or a game show episode.
His lack of statesmanship once again showed
when he introduced the guy who hawks pillows on TV
They are both drug addicts,
the sniffing makes it plain to see.
These snake-oil salesman are two of a kind,
who have both been sued and fined
for their fraudulent representation
of their products to the nation.
tRump stole from a kids cancer charity,
among his many other deadly sins.
The press briefings are just ads to
his base to ensure that
#45 wins.

# The MyPillow Guy

He hugs his MyPillow like #45 hugs the flag,
they think they have the election in the bag.
The MyPillow guy says #45 was sent by the Lord.
He and #45 are both guilty of fraud.

MyPillow guy said that people should read the bible
but if they do those people are liable
to find out that #45 is the antithesis
of what Jesus stood for.
He's is more like the anti-Christ with the sign of the
beast on his head, as he just doesn't care about
the number of people who are dead.
The only numbers #45 cares about
are his ratings and the balance of his bank account.
MyPillow guy said that kids who complain
about school shootings just whine.
I hope that they both have read psalm 109.
My prayer for #45 is in my book,
**America Wake Up;**
Psalm 109 is not the one where the cup
runneth over, it's very much darker indeed,
and it's something that we really need.
It's a prayer that bad people will meet their demise,
and that people will soon realize that this fake presidency
with corruption is rife,
and soon #45 will be in jail for the rest of his life.

*"The best president this country has ever had."*

**-Mike Lindell, MyPillow Guy**

# Distraction From Action

#45 was too distracted
when the impeachment was enacted
to pay attention to the virus that was sweeping the nation.
But it didn't stop him from nine political rallies
and six golfing trips,
and all the lies that spew from his lips.
His impeachable offences are numerous, however,
the Republican party will never
allow one of their own to go down without a fight,
even knowing that they are not in the right.
The GOP, Greed Over People, shall not prevail
we must win the election without fail.
No matter who is the candidate,
that person and his or her running mate,
we must vote blue, no matter who.
For no one in our history of the USA
has been as destructive
as the resident of the White House today.

| Days in office | 100 | 200 | 300 | 400 | 500 | 600 | 700 | 800 | 821 |
|---|---|---|---|---|---|---|---|---|---|
| Trump | 19 | 44 | 73 | 94 | 110 | 144 | 154 | 164 | 170 |
| Obama | 1 | 12 | 24 | 29 | 38 | 50 | 55 | 62 | 65 |
| Difference | 18 | 32 | 49 | 65 | 72 | 94 | 99 | 102 | 105 |

**Trump vs Obama Golf Count**

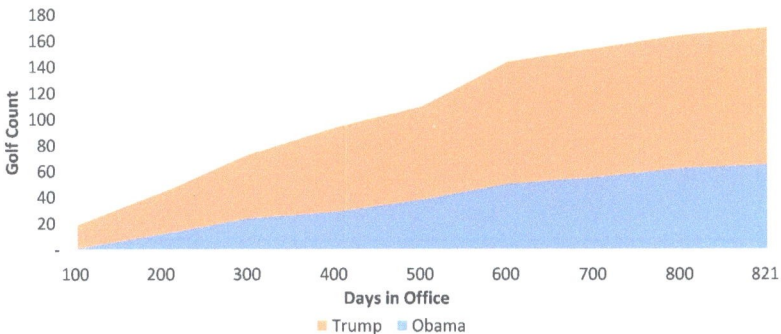

# A DePressing Problem

#45 is always attacking the press.
He has no class and no finesse.
He says they ask the wrong questions
when they just want the truth,
not a reproof,
from the liar-in-chief
whose lack of empathy is beyond belief.
He tells the reporters their questions are rude,
#45 has a terrible attitude.
When asked a question he doesn't like,
or doesn't want to answer,
his hatred for the press just grows
as though it were a cancer.
The reporters are just doing their jobs,
as #45 and his family robs the country of dignity,
and financial security.
Countries whose dictators suppress the press
are ultimately defeated by righteousness.

"They are evil people. The press, the media, they are bad people, and nobody lies like they do."

**-tRump**

# I'm #1

They say Nero fiddled while Rome burned
tRump just golfs, he hasn't learned.
He promises everything but delivers nothing,
and always finds someone else to blame.
Then he repeats the same process over and over again,
while trying to profit from the disease
and bringing the country to it's knees.
No matter the situation, this is #45's MO
as the number of people infected continues to grow.
In the middle of the nation's pandemic
tRump brags that he's Number One on a
social media page,
which puts many people in a rage.
If he's number one, the reason why
is because so many peoples' pages hate the guy.
He shows no concern for the sick and dying
and he's not even
trying to comfort
those in the health
professions,
who risk their lives
every day.
Which is why
people need to stay
at home and shelter
in place,
washing hands
frequently, and not
touching your face.

# The Good Doctor

Dr Fauci has been threatened by supporters of #45.
He has special security to make sure he stays alive.
He was doing his job, giving information that was correct,
but what else can you expect
from ignorant people who defend tRump's lies,
and don't try to disguise
their hatred of anyone who may disagree.
They are the same people who
have attacked Asians
with words and deeds reprehensible,
as though the Asians were all personally responsible
for the disease that is wildly spreading,
as this country is quickly heading
for deaths of epic proportion,
while #45 and his cronies
continue their efforts of extortion.
What's in it for me?
is the cry of the GOP.
While #45 in Jim Jones mode
tweets his insanity from his commode.

# Captain Courageous

Captain Brett Crozier knew what he had to do,
his priority was the safety of his crew.
Now of his position he has been relieved
because he did the right thing, as he believed,
even though he knew his job was at stake,
he just couldn't make
the decision to
let his crew continue to
get sick and die.
And that is why
his request to let his crew come to shore
to get treatment before
any more became infected
was met with derision, and his decision was suspected,
as he didn't follow proper protocol they said.
Is protocol more important than the number of dead?

Now the Captain,
as may have been
expected
is among the
number of
people infected.
For all those with
the virus we pray
for healing,
and justice for those
who this pandemic
were concealing.

# tRump World

In tRump World good is bad, and bad is good,
and it's not often understood.
If you report something wrong,
you will *not* be given a reward
but penalized, by America's greatest fraud.
On the other hand, if you are a cheat and a liar
the honor you'll receive couldn't be any higher.
A captain who put his crew's health before his job
was relived on his position,
yet Chief Gallagher a man who was guilty of
crimes of war, of killing civilians and posing for
photos with women and children, now dead,
was pardoned by #45 instead.
Sexual predators,
rogues and thieves
are men he calls friends,
and who he believes
are deserving of jobs in
his administration,
yet who are all robbing
this nation
of integrity and honesty
for personal gain,
although now some of
them in jail remain.
All tRump's casinos lost
money in gambling,
now he's known for his
constant incoherent rambling.

No money for small businesses and people in need,
but his space force program will go ahead at full speed.
Of this program he is really fond,
"To insanity and beyond!"
And one thing I'm willing to bet
that Captain Bone Spurs will be a great Space Cadet.
#45 says we have more virus
cases in the world than the rest
only because people continue to take the test.
What a totally ridiculous statement to make.
That's like saying women won't get pregnant
unless a test they take.
In this topsy turvy tRump World,
where nothing makes any sense
there is also Vice President Michael Pence,
and although he's not orange, he's white as the snow,
like#45 he's dangerous, and has to go.

# Oh Canada Eh?

Now #45 has made Justin Trudeau mad.
Canada is the best friend the USA has ever had.
It takes a lot to upset our Northern neighbors,
who work with Americans in their labors.
Yet, #45 refuses to send them equipment
that is needed ASAP
for their health works vitally.
Did #45 forget the way
the Canadians helped the USA
on that fateful day,
memorialized in the musical play
"Come From Away,"
on 9/11 when planes were stranded in Gander?
Yet #45 continues to pander
to dictators of countries far away,
and continues on his golf courses to play,
while deaths world-wide increase every day.

# Drug Pusher tRump

#45 keeps pushing a drug which he says will cure
the virus, but we know for sure that
he is lying once more,
as this drug has been lethal to some people
who have tried, with incorrect dosage, and then died.
For those with Lupus it's necessary for them to live,
but #45 doesn't give a hoot,
he's just interested in making more loot.
It's all about how much money he can make
and he doesn't care if the people who take
the drug live or die,
and the reason why, is #45 is heavily invested
in this drug, which hasn't been tested
or approved for the virus by the FDA,
yet his followers will take it anyway.
I'm sure it won't come as a great shock
that Guliani bought millions of dollars worth of stock
in this company which was paid
over a million dollars by Michael Cohen, #45's fixer,
before he went to jail, to have access to the elixir.

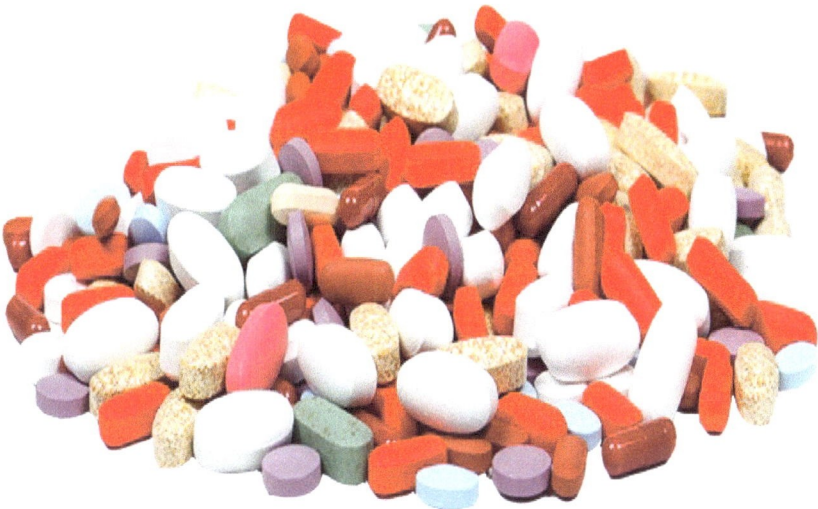

# Psych 101

Students learn in psychology 101
about projecting your fears onto another one.
#45 projects his own personal flaws
onto others because
he is guilty of everything he accuses
others of doing, as he abuses
his position of power
hour by hour.
This is psychology 101,
that's why he's called, "Don the Con."
He accuses everyone of all the dreadful deeds he's done.
He doesn't pay his debts, he lies all the time,
then accuses someone else of the crime.
A sexual predator, the lowest of the low,
in the history books he will go
as the worst president this country could know.
A master manipulator and wanna-be dictator,
destroying everything and everyone in his path,
as those who oppose him feel his wrath.
He insults journalists and tries to intimidate,
but wouldn't it be great
if some brave people would stand up and say,
"Why don't you tell us the truth today?"

---

"The most dangerous psychological

mistake is the projection of the shadow

onto others.                              **-Carl Jung**

---

# We Will Get Through

When I find myself moaning and complaining,
that at home I am remaining,
and that I have to spend weeks on end
in my house, and go outside only on the property to walk
and only talk to family and friends on the phone,
I realize that I'm not the only one,
and it isn't the first time this has been done.
In Europe during World War ll
there were people who
hid in attics and basements, and other tiny spaces,
and couldn't ever go out and show their faces.
Gypsies, homosexuals, the disabled and Jews
had to hide, they couldn't choose to walk outside.
And any others who the Nazis deemed inferior
had to hide in the interior of a room with many others,
separated from parents and sisters and brothers.
They hid in shelters as bombs rained down.
Many sent their children to the safety of another town.
Our lives are easy compared to what they all went through.
All we have to do, is wait it out in relative ease,
so when you feel down and frustrated, please,
remember those who lived through WW II,
they did it and you can do it too!

---

*I don't think of all the misery, but of the beauty that still remains."*

**-Ann Frank**

---

# 2020 Hindsight

#45 was warned about the virus many months before
it started spreading door to door.
A task force that was in place,
he disbanded... a total disgrace.
No responsibility would he take
as he said the virus was fake.
And Dr. Fauci, who tried to tell the real story,
was pushed aside for stealing tRump's glory.
It will go away very soon #45 said,
as the number of people sick or dead
began to increase with greater speed,
and the need grew for medical staff and supplies
while #45 just increased his lies.
In charge of the pandemic he put his son-in-law
who has no background in medicine, and what is more,
no qualifications whatsoever exist
in this grifting opportunist.
Now everyone is in the same boat,
but we need to be able to vote
out the dictator who is responsible
for actions reprehensible.

# Please Mr. Postman
## (or Woman)

#45 won't sign the bill that would bail out the US Postal
service, because he said votes by mail would fail to allow
"Repugnants" to win the election,
and so he prefers the selection
of votes that can be controlled with manipulation
by Putin and the Russian congregation
of trolls, and purveyors of fake news and misinformation.
That they will cheat again is a given,
the previous election was riven
with lies and obstruction
of justice, so tRump could win,
which is why this country, in all the states
finds itself in dire straits.
For over two hundred years the mail has been delivered
through wartime, and peace.
#45 wants to privatize so he can increase
his wealth and that of his partners in crime,
which he why he won't give the USPO one single dime!
Neither snow nor sleet, or rain or hail
can prevent the delivery of the mail.
The postal service is
vital to our
nation,
and we must
not allow the
tRump crime
organization
to stop the mail
delivery every day
across the whole of
the USA.

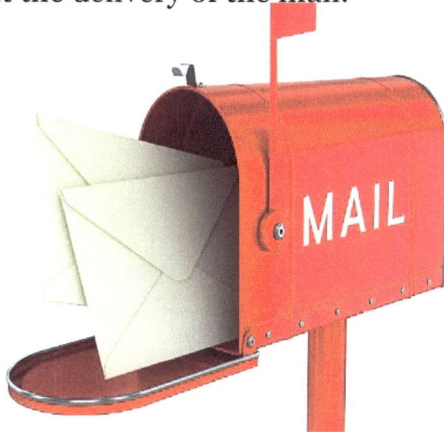

# Infection

Ivanka and Jared are in control
of the infectious disease patrol.
They're without experience or medical knowledge,
they didn't study it in college.
This must be breaking many laws,
and tRumps blatant nepotism will be the reason
for many more deaths in the coming season.
Follow the money and you will find
the tRump crime family behind
many of the laws he passes or not,
if he can't make money, that law is forgot.
He doesn't care what happens to the environment,
or how many people are sent to an early grave,
if it helps him and his buddies to save
money, and became even more wealthy,
at the risk of those who are unhealthy.
In a health crisis of epic proportion,
"he went to Jared," whose father was jailed for extortion.
The 1% are all #45 cares about,
they have the money and the clout
to keep him in his position as dictator,
but he must know that sooner or later
he will meet his demise, as those who
drank the Kool-Aid realize
that he, as every intelligent person knows,
is just an emperor without his clothes.

# Check Mate

#45 wanted his signature on all the stimulus checks,
that is really quite a laugh
as his signature looks just like a lie on a test of a polygraph.
Some of his cult members are deluded into thinking
that the money came from tRump himself
because "he's a billionaire"
it must be the Kool-Aid they've been drinking
because tRump "doesn't really care."

In some other countries the people receive
more money than in the USA.
Their checks come once a month
to make up for loss of pay.
Monthly stipends
to help make ends meet,
during the time of the economic defeat,
due to the virus crisis situation
that has affected every nation.

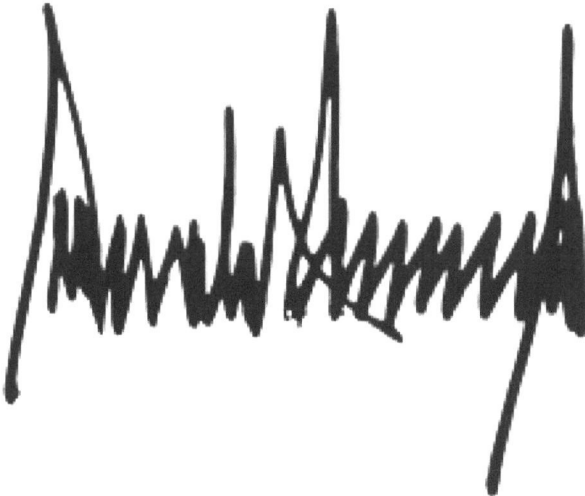

# Doctoring the Truth

I don't understand how Dr. Oz
could suggest opening the schools because,
he said only a small percent would die.
I don't know why
he would say such a thing,
and it has got me wondering
what if his child or grandchild was among the dead,
would he then regret what he has said?
What amount of deaths are acceptable?
only those who are most vulnerable?

Dr. Phil was heard to say
that car accidents kill people every day,
as do drownings in swimming pools,
so he wants to bend the rules
to allow people to go back to work.
This guy really is a jerk.
These remarks are quite outrageous,
car accidents and drownings are not contagious.
Their licenses should be taken away.

Doesn't the Hippocratic oath say,
"First do no harm?"
Their ignorance is cause for alarm.
They are willing to sacrifice lives for
the economy to thrive once more.

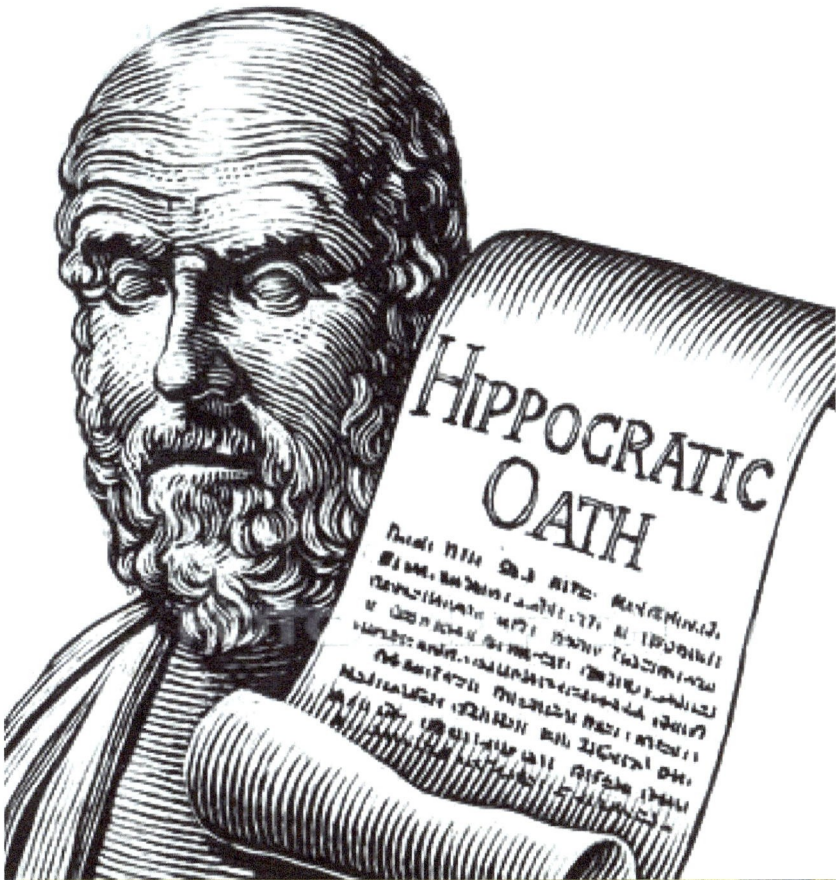

HIPPOCRATIC OATH

FIRST
DO NO HARM.

HIPPOCRATES

# The Life of O'Reilly

Bill O'Reilly has said those who are dead
due to the virus, were on their last legs.
He is among the dregs of society
to show such emotionless impropriety.
Lamenting the loss of economy
more than human lives
is indicative of a society
that already is in demise.
If you don't want to end up dead,
stay at home to stop the spread
of the virus that can kill,
without exception, people like Bill.
Remember to wash your hands frequently,
especially in November.
We must wash our hands of these viruses
and always remember
that diseases can spread rapidly
if you don't vote them out.
We must be rid of this crime family,
absolutely, without a doubt!

_"Many people who are dying, both here and around the world, were on their last legs anyway."_

**-Bill O'Reilly**

KEEP
CALM
AND
WASH
YOUR
HANDS
SG SUPERGUARD
ADVANCED
Hand
Sanitizer
Asseptgel
INSTANT Hand
Sanitizer
With Moisturizers
and Aloe Vera
Pears
TRANSPARENT SOAP
NET WT. 3.5 OZ (100 g)
Gentle Care

# WHO?

#45 defunded the World Health Organization
in his great determination
to punish them, as he didn't pay attention
to their December declaration,
that the virus needed swift action
from the USA,
to prevent a pandemic which is happening today.
If tRump had not defunded the CDC
and ignored the warnings of scientists,
who know better than he,
and the task forces put in place
by administrations previously,
both Republican and Democrat.
But #45 thinks he knows better than that,
and said it was a hoax, Democrats' jokes,
he said the virus was just "fake news folks."
It was just a plot to make him look bad, he said,
and there are only a small number of dead.
It will go away soon, you will see
that the pandemic is only a conspiracy.

# Justice For All?

I have a strong sense of justice,
of knowing what's wrong and what's right,
and when I see an injustice
I know that I have to fight.
White protester have been compared to
Rosa Parks, a black woman who
refused to give up her seat on a bus,
in a fight for racial equality for all of us.

How can these idiots be compared
to someone whose legacy is shared
in studies of America's history,
to me that is a mystery.
Rosa Parks didn't carry a gun,
she protested peacefully
like everyone
who followed the examples of MLK,
who asked himself what would Jesus say,
and what would Jesus do,
in situations with protesters who
claim to be Christians, yet behave in a way
that Christ would rebuke, if he were here today.

# Liberation?

"Your second amendment in under siege. Liberate,"
tweeted the con man whose words are fueled by hate,
who is inciting an overthrow of three states,
Minnesota, Michigan and Virginia.
Marching with confederate and Nazi flags
and demonstrating,
the people of these states are not negotiating,
but demanding freedom from the laws
which are for their own health and protection, because
they risk spreading the virus to all who are there,
although obviously they "really don't care."
As attacking women and minorities is happening again.
Our votes do not seem to count anymore
with reports of tampering with voting machines,
and Russian interference by any means,
welcomed by our traitor in chief
whose hubris is beyond belief!
Protesters want to go back to work and congregate
on the streets, like the college kids on
spring break, who didn't take
the shelter in place edict seriously at all,
and frocked on the beach
spreading the virus to one and all.
Now they will pay the price,
and their grandparents and others will sacrifice
their lives for just a few days fun
of playing on the beach in the sun.

*"... He lives in the illusion that he's admirable
in some way, yet he stand for everything that
is NOT admirable in American society."*

**- Roger Waters, on tRump**

# Cult #45

Although catching a virus is not what you planned,
it's like closing your parachute before you land,
or quitting your antibiotics when you feel better,
and not following doctor's orders to the letter.
I understand it's very frustrating,
these many months of endless waiting,
and like many others your income is gone,
so it's your savings you're relying upon.
You will work again when the virus has left,
without leaving your family and friends bereft.
Going out in public without a cover on
your face,  is irresponsible and a total disgrace.
Not practicing self-control has a domino effect,
and many other's lives will be wrecked.
They are all part  of the cult #45
and many of them  soon won't be alive.

# The Fixer

Now Michael Cohen is getting out of jail
and is writing a book with the true tale
of how he helped tRump to flaunt the law.
He will spill the beans and what is more
he was #45's fixer for many years,
and although Cohen hasn't expressed any fears,
I doubt that tRump, the orange crook,
will allow the book to see the light of day.
I have a feeling he'll end up the same way
as Jeffrey Epstein before much longer.
I hope his publisher has rights that are stronger
than the reach of the tRump family of crime,
and that Cohen's book is featured on the cover of Time.

---

"If somebody does something Mr. Trump doesn't like, I do everything in my power to resolve it to Mr. Trump's benefit. If you do something wrong, I'm going to come at you, grab you by the neck and I'm not going to let go until I'm finished."

**-Michael Cohen**

---

# Keep The Faith

George Santayana many years ago said,
that those who don't learn from history are
bound to end up dead.
Although that isn't the exact quote,
history is repeating, and has us by the throat.
In 1918 a pandemic swept the world and nation
and people who survived had lost their determination
to stay inside, so when the first World War ended
in the autumn of that year,
people took to the streets and put aside their fear
to celebrate the end of the war, however,
it was a shortsighted and foolish endeavor,
as the second wave of the pandemic spread
and left many more people dead,
even more than had died in the war.
So listen to this warning and take heed,
social distancing is what you need
to stay safe and well
from this terrible virus from Hell.

*"Those who do not remember the past are doomed to repeat it."*

**-George Santayana**

# HELP!

Spending months alone in the house
with your partner or your spouse,
can make you want to go outside and say
"Give me the virus so I can die today!"

But seriously, this is perhaps the
greatest challenge
a relationship can take,
and we all have to make
allowances for our partners who
are now beyond annoying, this is true.

Not talking to each other is the perfect way
as we struggle to get through another day.
Watching TV so we don't have to talk,
or go outside and take a walk.
But don't go off your property line
without a mask, and you will be fine.

Staying calm and practice meditation
will help relieve the irritation.
Take deep breaths and count to ten,
and pray we can all survive until when
this pandemic is over and we are free.

Although I have a feeling that we shall see,
many babies being born, and lots of divorce,
but not with the same couples of course!

# A Silver Lining

This pandemic has a surprising silver lining,
the environment is improving, and we are finding
crystal clear waters and skies that are blue,
air so clean in India they now have a view
of the Himalayan mountains,
that once were hidden by air pollution so thick,
that the smoke and smog made people sick.
In the oceans many fish can be seen,
because the water is now so clean.
Although there are still a few thoughtless people out there,
there are fewer cars on the road, fewer planes in the air
fewer ships on the ocean,
and more people who show their love and devotion
to neighbors and strangers they don't even know,
by shopping or preparing a meal
so that shut in people don't have to feel
that they are alone as they shelter in place,
the friendliness brings a smile to their face.

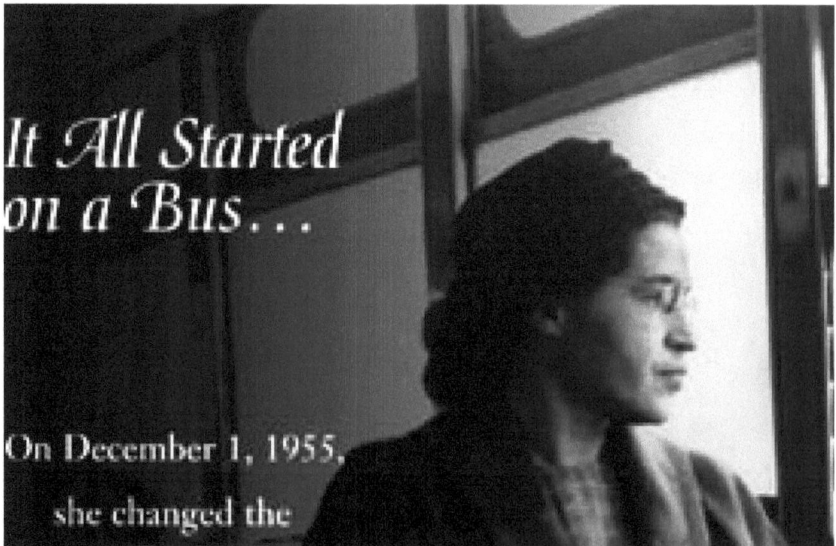

It All Started on a Bus...

On December 1, 1955, she changed the

# WW or AA?

When this is over where will I go first,
to appease my hunger and quench my thirst;
will it be to lose some weight,
or will no more drinking be my fate?
I've been eating three meals a day
ever since we've been locked away.
As we shelter here in place
I've been happily feeding my face.
Every day when the clock chimes five
my happy hour comes alive.
Gin or vodka, red wine or white,
I'll give in without a fight.
It doesn't matter whether I'm making meat or fish
whatever alcohol I serve goes with any dish.
It doesn't matter what I wear
as I'm not going anywhere.
Everything is canceled, I have no place to go,
nobody will see me, and so
I haven't worn jewelry in a very long time
nor shopped for new clothes with friends of mine.
I don't bother to paint my nails
or do much with my hair.
By the time this pandemic is over
will anyone still care?

# In The Wild

The animals are now roaming where humans fear to tread.
The areas where once were filled with people
now have animals instead.
Pandas in zoos, whose keepers were waiting for them to
mate, now that the zoos are empty,
the pandas decided it's not too late.
Who needs an audience when you're procreating?
That makes common animal sense in mating.
Not only in national parks is the wildlife expanding,
everywhere animals live they are demanding
a source of food as they freely roam
far from their natural comfort zone.
Coyotes in San Francisco, goats in Wales
all on the streets wagging their tails.
Macaque monkeys in Thailand, in the temple,
Phra Prang Sam Yot,
the starving monkeys no food have they got,
as once by tourists they were fed.
They now look in deserted towns to seek their daily bread.
It used to be that people encroached on animal's habitat,
now the tables are turned, and it seems that
birds in the air and fish in the sea
are increasing exponentially.

---

*"The successful natural mating process today is extremely exciting for all of us, as the chance of pregnancy via natural mating is higher than by artificial insemination."*

**-Michael Boos**
**Executive Director at Ocean Park Zoo in Hong Kong**

# Brave New World

There will be millions of people who died,
and millions more who have mourned and cried,
by the time this world-wide pandemic is done.
Many jobs will be lost, many incomes gone,
but we still have to carry on.
The biggest cities have the greatest loss,
the minorities and the poor
will be the ones to suffer the most,
sadly, just as they have before.
The medical professionals were the first to heed the call
Just like on 9/11 when first responders saw the towers fall.
Putting others before self
is the greatest gift that one can give,
saving lives, donating food so that others can live.
There will be so many people who
will need help just to make ends meet.
Everyone who was living paycheck to paycheck
will need help getting back on their feet.
We have to adapt as the wildlife has,
only the strong survive,
those who practiced social distancing
will be the ones still alive.

---

"It's not the strongest of the species that survive, nor the most intelligent, but the one most responsive to change."

-Charles Darwin

---

# R.I.P.

Six feet apart is better than six feet under,
the ignorance of some people makes me wonder
what on earth is wrong with them.
Rest at home is better than rest in peace, don't you think?
How much Kool-Aid did these folks drink?
There is blood on the hands of all who denied,
and protested the rules to stay inside,
and as a result so many have died.
There will be people who will catch the virus
because they have to treat
those idiots who took to the street.
An oath was taken by the medical profession
to do no harm, and make no concession
to those who put others' lives in danger,
but to treat everyone, including the stranger.
Don't risk being infected by the second wave,
which is sure to come if we don't behave
in a manner that takes into consideration
everybody in the nation.
Selfish actions just exacerbate
the evolution of our fate.

# LieSol Don

Will they drink a martini laced with bleach
as they all party on the beach,
or inject themselves with products that disinfect?
I think that we can now expect
tRump supporters to try these cures that he has espoused
in this pandemic, which he "has aroused."
Clorox or Lysol or the store's own brand,
the results are the same for this pathetic band
of tRump cult followers who don't understand
that they have swallowed the Kool-Aid along with his lies,
and will follow his ravings until their demise.
#45 was impeached not "in bleached."
Another fact that is alarming,
the term for disinfectant inside the body, is embalming.
From the virus they possibly may die,
but from painful poisoning if they try
these so-called cures from a snake oil seller,
a ruthless, greedy, obnoxious old fella.
No wonderful pearls of wisdom are these,
but toxic words from a man with a mental disease.

---

*"And then I see the disinfectant, where it knocks it out in one minute and is there a way you can do something like that, by injection inside, or almost a cleaning."*

**- Donald Trump, to Bill Bryan, head of science and technology at Homeland Security**

---

# Go Directly To Jail

Stock market fraud by politicians in the know
should be punished; off to jail they should go.
They dumped stocks by insider trading
because they knew that the market was fading.
Other celebrities have gone to jail
because to report income they did fail,
or they cheated in admission to college,
as their children lacked the knowledge
to attend on merit of their own.
Members of the tRump administration
who have helped him to bleed this nation dry,
when we should be asking why
they will bail out every big corporation,
but small businesses receive no compensation?

# Human Rights

When indigenous people and minorities demonstrate
they have been met with expressions of hate,
water hoses, attack dogs, clubs and tear gas,
but white people are always given a pass
when they demonstrate
on the steps of the capital of a state,
with guns and flags, which are symbols of hate.

People who want to get a haircut and paint their nails
don't seem to get it; that this fails
to stop the virus from spreading and expanding.
It is beyond their understanding
that the virus is air borne and will spread,
until many people on this planet are dead.
It's better be at home than in Intensive Care,
which endangers lives of the medical workers there.
Prevention is easier than finding a cure,
which may take a long time before
a vaccine, or some other medication,
is available for dissemination.

---

*"One's philosophy is not best expressed in words; its expressed in the choices one makes."*

**- Eleanor Roosevelt**

---

# In Breeding

You'd have to be a wackadoodle
to hire a breeder of labradoodles
to head up a medical task force.
This man had of course
donated to tRump's campaign,
and even if you only have half a brain
you'd realize that he has no background scientific,
although tRump may think that he's terrific.
Agent Orange says he has a big brain,
yet he wanted to nuke a hurricane,
then changed it's direction with a sharpie on a map,
everybody knows he's full of crap.

#45 is so "bragadocious"
and his lies are so atrocious.
He said that if you rake the forest floor
you won't have wildfires anymore.
Windmills cause cancer was another thing he said,
if that was true all the Dutch people would be dead.
He claims to know more
than anyone about every single topic,
but it's obvious that his view of the world is 100% myopic.

---

*"If you have a windmill anywhere near your house, congratulations, your property went down 75% in value, and they say the noise causes cancer."*

— **Donald Trump**

---

# The tRump Virus

#45 just continues to lie
as hundreds of thousands of Americans die.
No matter where this virus originated,
#45 has only complicated it's growth and spread
by the foolish things that he has said.
People of Asian origin living in the USA,
have been attacked by racist people
who listen to what Agent Orange has to say.
A man so stupid he looked directly at a solar eclipse.
You know he is lying when he's moving his lips.
He said that windmills cause cancer
and the virus was a hoax.
People who believe him are just ignorant folks.
He said to prevent forest fires you must rake the leaves
is there anyone who still believes
a word that comes out of his orange face?
His lack of leadership is a total disgrace!

# Home Grown Terrorists

Men protesting quarantine armed to the teeth,
hiding their insecurities underneath.
They seem think that sheltering in place is a liberal plot,
there is not one ounce of common sense among the lot.
#45 words incites them into a frenzied mob,
making them believe that it is now their job
to protest safety rules put in place,
gathering close together, with no mask upon each face.

These fools don't seem to comprehend
that the virus will infect them in the end.
Some will recover, some will die,
but medical workers, who risk their own health every day,
have taken an oath to heal, and just cannot say,
"I refuse to treat those who protest."
They just carry on and do their best.
They are all committed
to help everyone who is admitted
into the hospital for care,
even though it isn't fair.

Although they are not known by the name,
these protesters are terrorists just the same!
Although I didn't expect much from his presidency,
I never thought I'd live to see
this country torn by such chaos and division,
bigotry, hatred and derision.
There has never been a presidency
so riddled with toxicity.

Not since the Civil War have families
disagreed to such an extent,
that holidays that were meant
to bring us together to celebrate,
now are occasions when people hesitate,
and are afraid to express
their opinions unless
they offend the other's point of view.
Whatever happened to
relationships where people could disagree,
yet not end their friendship permanently?

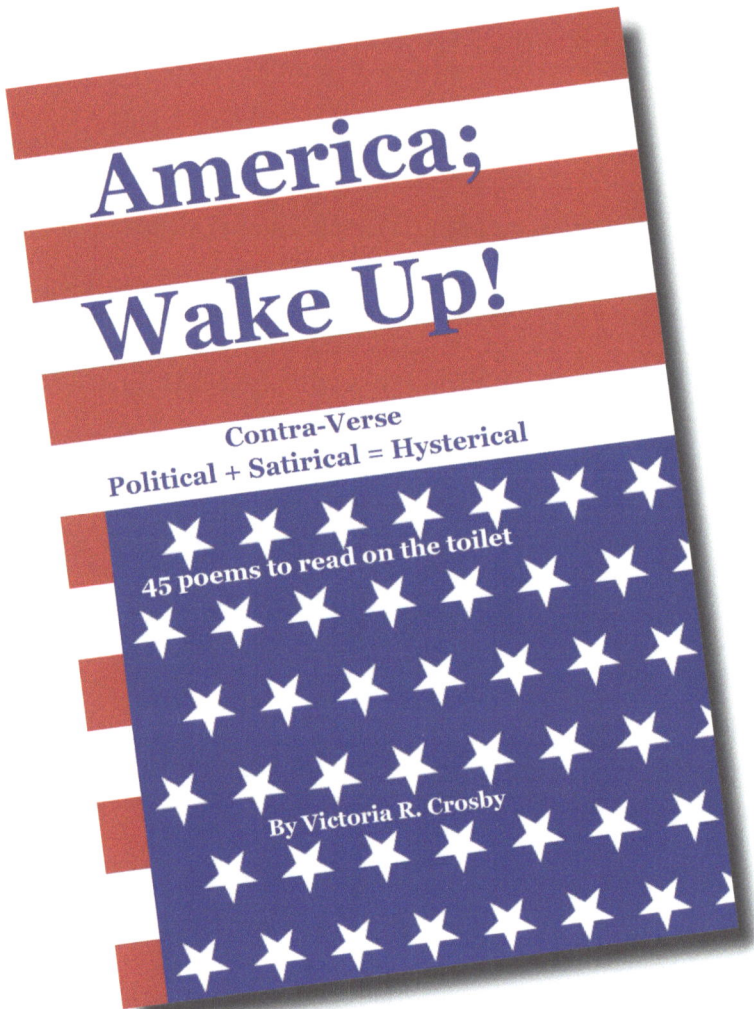

**Also by Victoria Crosby, "America; Wake Up!"**

Sometimes you have to laugh to keep from crying. This is why we need political satire, to laugh and cry at human foibles. Written by an acclaimed poet and journalist, whose work ranges from humorous to inspirational, and who, as a political activist herself, has supported many humanitarian causes. With quotes and tweets from philosophers, religious leaders, writers, presidents and dictators, and photographs on topics from the serious to the absurd, this poetry collection chronicles the years 2016-2019 in rhyming verse.

⭐⭐⭐⭐⭐ **What a Treasure!**

This book arrived the day before impeachment, providing joy and clarity, uplifting my solemn mood. It's smart, sassy and fun: like therapy for Trump victims! For instance, "Malice At The Palace:" describes his boorish visit with the Queen, reminding us of his photo projected on the London Tower, "where many a traitor lost their head and power." her poem about Independence Day brought a tear to my eye: "How can I celebrate today, when children continued to be locked away." Outrage is marked by compassion, spiced with wit and wisdom. What a treasure.                    **- Sarah A. Phd. NY**

⭐⭐⭐⭐⭐ **Terrific Political Satire**

Wonderful and biting political satire done to a very high level. Perfect gift for anyone who needs a good antidote to the times we are living through.

The poems are all clever and funny, never a dull moment!

**- Marian B. SC**

⭐⭐⭐⭐⭐ **America Needs to Wake Up**

It has been said that if you don't laugh you'll cry. Thanks to Victoria Crosby's clever, and on point poems, the reader is offered the opportunity to laugh.

Anyone searching for someone who feels their pain, and sees the insanity and danger of #45, will welcome the acknowledgement of their own feelings as well.

Victoria Crosby put down in prose what we are feeling - It's a good read!                                                **- Mark B. NY**

⭐⭐⭐⭐⭐ **I Gave a Dozen as Gifts**

Provocative, informative, and supremely entertaining, this collection of clever poems gives a clear voice to those of us who are troubled by our current political climate. I just bought a dozen copies to give as gifts.

**- Beverly Hurwitz MD, author of**
**"Nobody Else's Business" and "Is the Cat Lady Crazy?" UT**

# About The Author

Victoria Crosby is a journalist, writing for newspapers and magazines for more than twenty years. Her motivational and inspirational poetry has been featured in many publications, and on her weekly radio show, "Oasis." Her political satire poetry column, "Per-Verse," was featured in the now defunct Long Island Voice, an offshoot of The Village Voice.

As Poet Laureate for the City of Glen Cove since 1994, she has written and read at many special occasions, for individuals and organizations in Glen Cove, and the Long Island community at large.

Victoria is on the board of many non-profit organizations, including the Historic Royal Palaces in the UK, and the Glen Cove Arts Council, a charity she founded in 2006.

She has also written the life story, in rhyming verse, of Elvis Presley, which is featured on WHPC 90.3, twice a year on the anniversary of his birth and death. She performs her humorous and motivational poetry for many groups, and performs her Elvis, Frank Sinatra, and other celebrities life story poetry with singers, as part of a group called, "Poetry in Motion."

Born and raised in Cheshire, UK, with elementary and high school education in England, educator and music teacher Victoria Crosby received her Master's Degree from Long Island University.

www.ingramcontent.com/pod-product-compliance
Lightning Source LLC
Chambersburg PA
CBHW042107110426
42742CB00033BA/18